SCHOLASTIC

MW01205630

MATH PRACTICE

New York • Toronto • London • Auckland • Sydney
Mexico City • New Delhi • Hong Kong • Buenos Aires

Teaching
Resources

Cover design by Jay Namerow
Interior illustrations by Jon Buller, Reggie Holladay, Anne Kennedy, Kathy Marlin, Bob Masheris, Sherry Neidigh, and Carol Tiernon
Interior design by Quack & Company

ISBN 0-439-81915-6

4 5 6 7 8 9 10 40   13 12 11 10 09

Table of Contents

Dear Parent:

Welcome to *1st Grade Math Practice!* This valuable tool is designed to help your child succeed in school. Scholastic, the most trusted name in learning, has been creating quality educational materials for school and home for nearly a century. And this resource is no exception.

Inside this book, you'll find colorful and engaging activity pages that will give your child the practice he or she needs to master essential skills, such as adding and subtracting, identifying shapes, telling time, measuring, and so much more.

To support your child's learning experience at home, try these helpful tips:

- Provide a comfortable, well-lit place to work, making sure your child has all the supplies he or she needs.

- Encourage your child to work at his or her own pace. Children learn at different rates and will naturally develop skills in their own time.

- Praise your child's efforts. If your child makes a mistake, offer words of encouragement and positive help.

- Display your child's work and celebrate his successes with family and friends.

We hope you and your child will enjoy working together to complete this workbook.

Happy learning!
The Editors

Number User

I use numbers to tell about myself.

1. _____
   MY STREET NUMBER

2. _____
   MY ZIP CODE

3. _____
   MY TELEPHONE NUMBER

4. _____
   MY BIRTHDAY

5. _____
   MY AGE

6. _____
   MY HEIGHT AND WEIGHT

7. _____
NUMBER OF PEOPLE IN MY FAMILY

I CAN COUNT UP TO

8. _____

Flowers in a Pot

Count the dots in the boxes. Then color the matching number word.

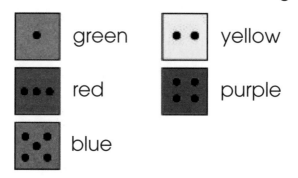

green
yellow
red
purple
blue

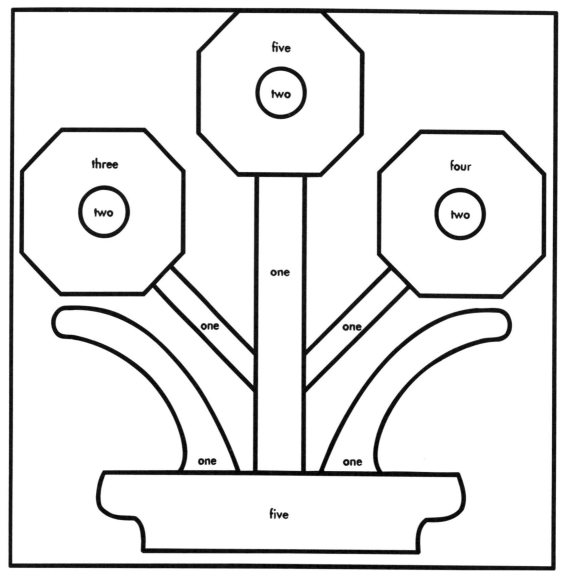

Use bright colors to draw a pot of flowers on another sheet of paper.

Color the Basket

Count the number of dots or triangles in each shape. Then use the Color Key to tell you what color to make each shape. (For example, a shape with 7 dots will be colored green.)

Extra: On a separate sheet of paper, draw a basket filled with six things you would carry in it.

Color Key
6 = yellow
7 = green
8 = brown
9 = red
10 = orange

Mystery Critter

I climb up the side of walls and never fall.

I am a fast runner and have a very long tail. Who am I? _____

To find out, connect the numbers in order from 0 to 48.

Frog School

At Frog School, Croaker Frog and his friends sit on lily pads.

Are there enough lily pads for all the frogs in Croaker's class?
Yes ____   No ____

Draw lines to match the frogs with the lily pads.

 How many frogs need lily pads? _____

Odd and Even Patterns

A pattern can have two things repeating.
This is called an "AB" pattern.

1. Look around the classroom. What "AB" patterns do you see?
   Draw one "AB" pattern in the box.

2. Use red and blue crayons to color the numbers in the chart using
   an "AB" pattern.

Hundred's Chart

1	2	3	4	5	6	7	8	9	10
11	12	13	14	15	16	17	18	19	20
21	22	23	24	25	26	27	28	29	30
31	32	33	34	35	36	37	38	39	40
41	42	43	44	45	46	47	48	49	50
51	52	53	54	55	56	57	58	59	60
61	62	63	64	65	66	67	68	69	70
71	72	73	74	75	76	77	78	79	80
81	82	83	84	85	86	87	88	89	90
91	92	93	94	95	96	97	98	99	100

Use this rule:
   1 = red
   2 = blue
   3 = red
   4 = blue, and so on

The blue numbers are
even numbers. They can
be split evenly into 2
whole numbers.

The red numbers are **odd
numbers**. They cannot be
split evenly into 2 whole
numbers.

Sign Shape

Street signs come in different shapes. Use string to form the shapes below. Answer the questions below about the shapes, too.

What shape is this sign? _____

How many sides does it have? _____

What shape is this sign? _____

How many sides does it have? _____

What shape is this sign? _____

How many sides does it have? _____

What shape is this sign? _____

How many sides does it have? _____

Bird Feeder Geometry

It's spring! The birds are coming back. Kwaku and his mother made two bird feeders.

What shapes can you find on their feeders? Write your ideas on

the lines. _____

_____

Shape Study

"Symmetry" exists when the two halves of something are mirror images of each other.

Look at the pictures below. Color those that show symmetry.
(Hint: Imagine the pictures are folded on the dotted lines.)

Complete the drawings below. Connect the dots to show the other half. (Hint: The pictures are symmetrical!)

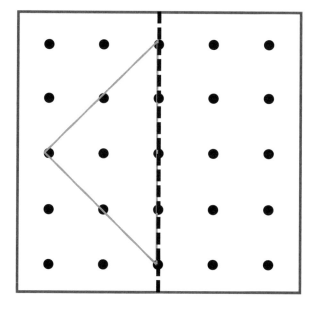

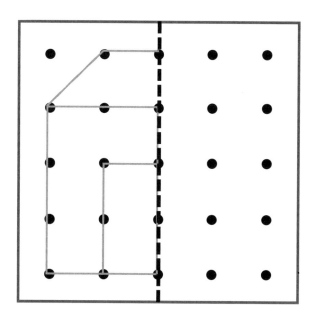

Pattern Block Design

How many total pieces are in this pattern block design?

$$2 + 2 + 1 = \underline{\hspace{2cm}}$$

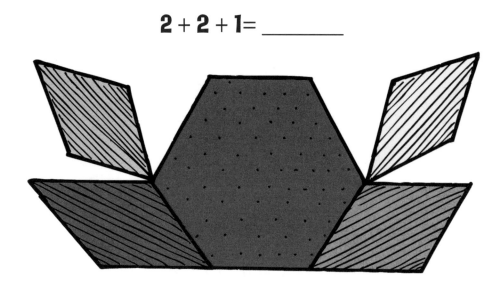

Now make your own design by drawing 5 pattern blocks. Connect the blocks to form a pattern different from the one above. You may want to use a block pattern more than once.

Write an equation to show how many of each shape you used.

Equation: _____

Lovely Ladybugs

Write a number sentence to show how many spots each ladybug has.

_1_ + _2_ = _3_

____ + ____ = ____

____ + ____ = ____

____ + ____ = ____

____ + ____ = ____

____ + ____ = ____

____ + ____ = ____

____ + ____ = ____

____ + ____ = ____

Color the ladybug with the greatest number of spots red.

Color the ladybug with the least number of spots blue.

Scholastic Teaching Resources

Clowning Around

Add. Color the picture using the color code.

Color Code

1	pink
2	white
3	black
4	brown
5	purple
6	green
7	blue
8	orange
9	yellow
10	red

$5 + 2 =$

$6 + 3 =$

$\begin{array}{r} 4 \\ + 5 \\ \hline \end{array}$

$\begin{array}{r} 5 \\ + 0 \\ \hline \end{array}$

$\begin{array}{r} 2 \\ + 3 \\ \hline \end{array}$

$\begin{array}{r} 7 \\ + 2 \\ \hline \end{array}$

$\begin{array}{r} 4 \\ + 4 \\ \hline \end{array}$

$2 + 5 =$

$3 + 2 =$

$\begin{array}{r} 4 \\ + 3 \\ \hline \end{array}$

$\begin{array}{r} 3 \\ + 3 \\ \hline \end{array}$

$\begin{array}{r} 1 \\ + 0 \\ \hline \end{array}$

$\begin{array}{r} 4 \\ + 2 \\ \hline \end{array}$

$\begin{array}{r} 0 \\ + 1 \\ \hline \end{array}$

$\begin{array}{r} 5 \\ + 1 \\ \hline \end{array}$

$4 + 1 =$

$\begin{array}{r} 6 \\ + 2 \\ \hline \end{array}$

$\begin{array}{r} 2 \\ + 1 \\ \hline \end{array}$

$7 + 0 =$

$\begin{array}{r} 3 \\ + 0 \\ \hline \end{array}$

$\begin{array}{r} 3 \\ + 5 \\ \hline \end{array}$

$5 + 5 =$

$6 + 1 =$

$\begin{array}{r} 1 \\ + 1 \\ \hline \end{array}$

$7 + 3 =$

$3 + 1 =$

Beautiful Bouquets

Look at the number on each bow. Draw more flowers to match the number written on the bow.

Color the bows with an even number yellow.

Color the bows with an odd number purple.

Telephone Math

What kind of phone never rings? _____

To find out, solve the addition problems. Then use the code on the telephone to replace your answers with letters. The first one has been done for you.

$$\begin{array}{r} 6 \\ + 2 \\ \hline 8 \end{array}$$ __A__

$$\begin{array}{r} 5 \\ + 1 \\ \hline \end{array}$$ _____

$$\begin{array}{r} 4 \\ + 4 \\ \hline \end{array}$$ _____

$$\begin{array}{r} 3 \\ + 6 \\ \hline \end{array}$$ _____

$$\begin{array}{r} 3 \\ + 0 \\ \hline \end{array}$$ _____

$$\begin{array}{r} 3 \\ + 4 \\ \hline \end{array}$$ _____

$$\begin{array}{r} 2 \\ + 2 \\ \hline \end{array}$$ _____

$$\begin{array}{r} 2 \\ + 1 \\ \hline \end{array}$$ _____

$$\begin{array}{r} 1 \\ + 1 \\ \hline \end{array}$$ _____

$$\begin{array}{r} 0 \\ + 1 \\ \hline \end{array}$$ _____

 Write your telephone number in letters using the phone code above.

_____

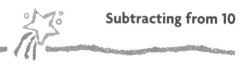

Juggling Act

Cross out. Write how many are left.

4 − 2 = _____

3 − 1 = __2__

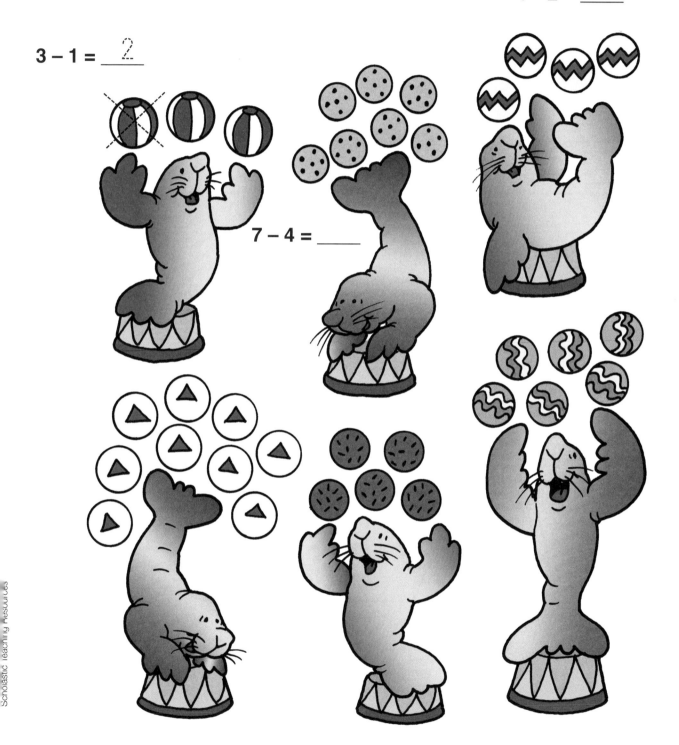

7 − 4 = _____

9 − 6 = _____   5 − 3 = _____   6 − 5 = _____

High Flyer

Do the subtraction problems.

If the answer is 1 or 2, color the shape red.
If the answer is 3 or 4, color the shape blue.
If the answer is 5 or 6, color the shape yellow.
If the answer is 7 or 8, color the shape green.
If the answer is 9, color the shape black.
Color the other shapes the colors of your choice.

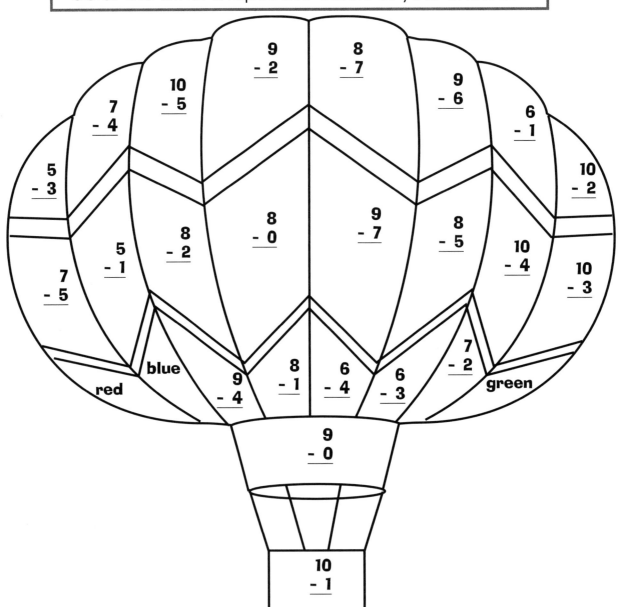

Trucking Along

Subtract. Color the picture using the color code.

Color Code

0	white
1	brown
2	black
3	green
4	purple
5	orange
6	yellow
7	blue
8	red

$9 - 2$

$7 - 6 =$

$9 - 1 =$

$8 - 4 =$ $7 - 3 =$ $6 - 2 =$

$10 - 6$

$9 - 5$

$1 - 1$

$4 - 4 =$

$5 - 2$

$10 - 7$

$10 - 2 =$

$10 - 4 =$

$8 - 2$

$10 - 9$

$6 - 3 =$

$9 - 4 =$

$9 - 3$

$9 - 7 =$

$10 - 8 =$

$7 - 5 =$

$9 - 6$

$8 - 2 =$

$4 - 3$

$9 - 1$

Night Lights

Subtract. Connect the dots from greatest to least.

$10 - 3 = \boxed{}$ •

$9 - 1 = \boxed{}$ •

$8 - 2 = \boxed{}$

$10 - 1 = \boxed{}$ •

• $9 - 4 = \boxed{}$

$10 - 0 = \boxed{}$ •

• $7 - 3 = \boxed{}$

$5 - 3 = \boxed{}$ •

$6 - 5 = \boxed{}$ •

• $8 - 5 = \boxed{}$

Subtract. Connect the dots from least to greatest.

$10 - 0 = \boxed{}$ • - - • $9 - 8 = \boxed{}$

• $7 - 5 = \boxed{}$

$10 - 1 = \boxed{}$ •

• $10 - 7 = \boxed{}$

$10 - 2 = \boxed{}$ •

 The top picture gives off its own light. Color this picture orange. The bottom picture reflects light from the sun. Color this picture yellow.

$7 - 0 = \boxed{}$ •

• $6 - 2 = \boxed{}$

$9 - 3 = \boxed{}$ •

• $9 - 4 = \boxed{}$

Measuring Up

People didn't always measure with rulers. Long ago, Egyptians and other peoples measured objects with body parts. Try it!

A "digit" is the width of your middle finger at the top joint where it bends.

How many digits long is:

a pair of scissors? _____

a math book? _____

a crayon? _____

A "palm" is the width of your palm.

How many palms long is:

a telephone book? _____

your desk? _____

a ruler? _____

A "span" is the length from the tip of your pinkie to the tip of your thumb when your hand is wide open.

How many spans long is:

a broom handle? _____

a table? _____

a door? _____

Penguin Family on Parade

The penguin family is part of the winter parade. They need to line up from shortest to tallest. Give them a hand! Use a ruler to measure each penguin. Label each penguin with its height. Then write the name of each penguin in size order, from shortest to tallest.

Paul
Height:

_____

inches

Peter
Height:

_____

inches

Patty
Height:

_____

inches

Petunia
Height:

_____

inches

Size Order:

_____   _____   _____   _____

(smallest)   (tallest)

Look and Learn

Look at each picture. Estimate how long you think it is. Then measure each picture with a ruler. Write the actual length in inches.

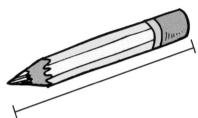

Estimate: _____ inches
Actual: _____ inches

Estimate: _____ inches
Actual: _____ inches

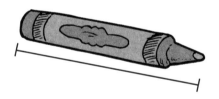

Estimate: _____ inches
Actual: _____ inches

Estimate: _____ inches
Actual: _____ inches

Practice measuring other things in the room with a ruler.

Centimeters

Things can be measured using centimeters. Get a ruler that measures in centimeters. Measure the pictures of the objects below.

book	**book**
_____ centimeters	_____ centimeters
straw	**marker**
_____ centimeters	_____ centimeters
5 cubes	**10 cubes**
_____ centimeters	_____ centimeters
shoe	**hand**
_____ centimeters	_____ centimeters

Hop to It: Add and Subtract

Add or subtract. Trace the number line with your finger to check your work.

Examples: **4 + 5 = _____**   **4 − 2 = _____**

Start on **4**.   Start on **4**.

Move **5** 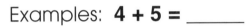 right.   Move **2** 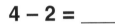 left.

7 − 3 = _____	9 − 6 = _____	2 + 0 = _____
5 + 5 = _____	8 − 7 = _____	4 + 3 = _____
10 − 4 = _____	6 + 2 = _____	7 − 2 = _____

 Circle the answer to each question.

What direction did move to add?   left   or   right

What direction did move to subtract?   left   or   right

Mitten Matchup

Add or subtract. Draw a line to match mittens with the same answer.

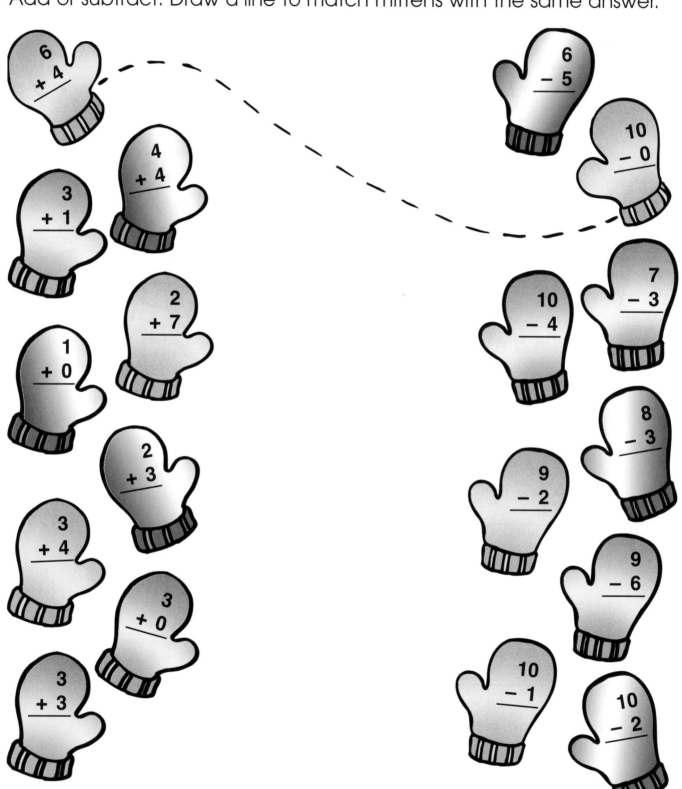

Blast Off

Add or subtract. Then use the code to answer the riddle below.

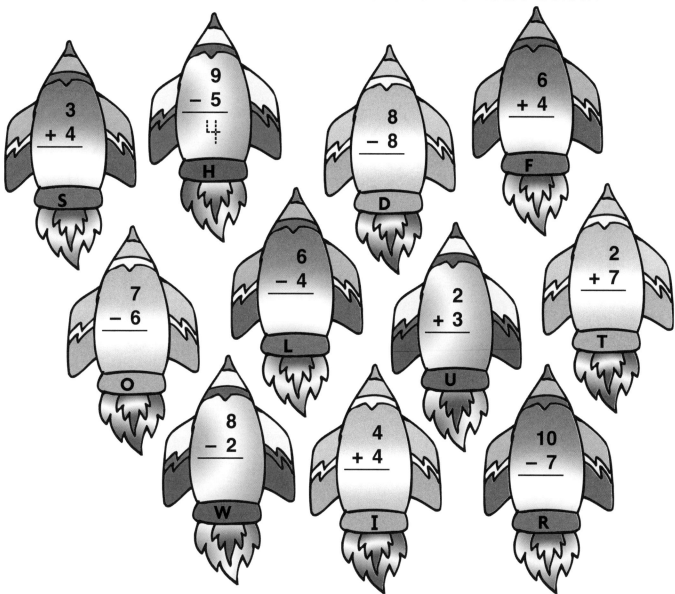

$3 + 4$ **S**

$9 - 5$ 4 **H**

$8 - 8$ **D**

$6 + 4$ **F**

$7 - 6$ **O**

$6 - 4$ **L**

$2 + 3$ **U**

$2 + 7$ **T**

$8 - 2$ **W**

$4 + 4$ **I**

$10 - 7$ **R**

How is an astronaut's job unlike any other job?

____ ____ ____   ____ ____ ____   ____ ____ '
 8   9   7   1   5   9   1   10

____ H ____ ____   ____ ____ ____ ____ ____ !
 9   4   8   7   6   1   3   2   0

Shapes on a Snake

Add or subtract.

A. 🩷6 + ⬭4 = __10__

B. ⬜ – ◇ = _____

C. ⬤ – ⬡ = _____

D. ⬭ + 🩷 = _____

E. ▯ + ⬡ = _____

F. ⬡ + ⬡ = _____

G. ◇ + ⬡ = _____

H. 🩷 + ⬭ = _____

I. △ – ▯ = _____

J. ⬜ – ⬡ = _____

Planes . . . Trains . . .

Add or subtract.

A.
There are **7** cars in the parking lot. Then **3** more cars park there, too. How many cars are there in all in the lot?

__7__ ⊕ __3__ = __10__ cars

B.
There are **7** boxes on the truck. Then **4** boxes fall on the street. How many boxes are left on the truck?

____ + ____ = ____ boxes
      −

C.
There are **10** planes waiting on the runway. Then **6** planes take off. How many planes are left on the runway?

____ + ____ = ____ planes
      −

D.
There are **8** girls and **2** boys on the bus. How many more girls than boys are on the bus?

____ + ____ = ____ more girls
      −

E.
There are **5** people in the first car and **4** people in the second car. How many people in all?

____ + ____ = ____ people
      −

Out on the Town

Color a box on the graph for each item in the picture.

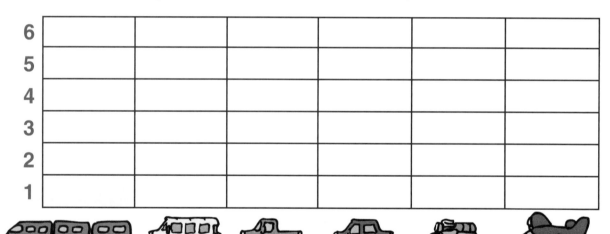

A. How many and  altogether? $6 \oplus 2 = 8$

B. How many and in all? ___ + ___ = ___

C. How many more than ? ___ + ___ = ___

Scholastic Teaching Resources

Five Senses

We learn about the world by using our 5 senses. The 5 senses are seeing, hearing, smelling, touching, and tasting.

Look at the pictures on the left side of the graph. Think about which of your senses you use to learn about it. Draw a checkmark in the box to show the senses used. (Hint: You might use more than one.)

	See	**Hear**	**Smell**	**Touch**	**Taste**
🐓					
☀					
🥤					
🌼					
🥁					

Now graph how many senses you used for each object.

5					
4					
3					
2					
1					

Rainbow Graph

Which color of the rainbow is your favorite? Color in the box for your favorite color. Have 5 friends color the boxes to show their favorite colors, too.

Which color is liked the most? _____

Which color is liked the least? _____

Are any colors tied? _____

Which ones? _____

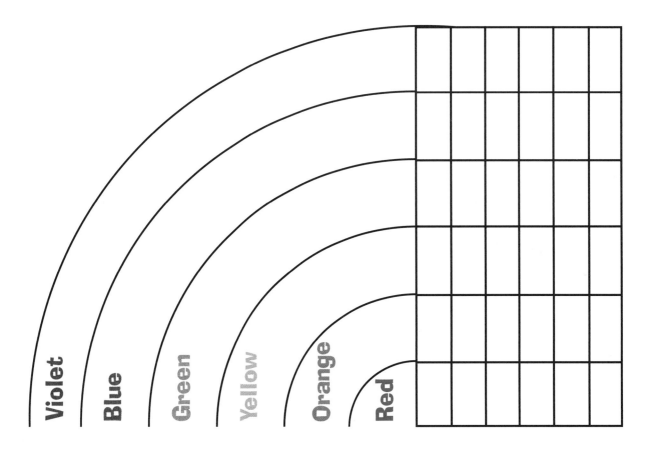

Leap on Over

Add. To show the frog's path across the pond, color each lily pad green if the sum is greater than 10.

10 + 1 =

6 + 4 =

6 + 9 =

5 + 2 =

7 + 0 =

5 + 5 =

9 + 2 =

10 + 4 =

3 + 7 =

7 + 6 =

4 + 3 =

5 + 4 =

3 + 8 =

2 + 2 =

8 + 8 =

 How many leaps did the frog take across the pond? _____

Scarecrow Sam

Why doesn't Scarecrow Sam tell secrets when he is near Farmer Joe's bean patch? _____

To find out the answer, add the numbers. Circle the pumpkins that have sums of 14, and write the letters that appear inside those pumpkins in the boxes below.

Ladybug Dots

Every year, ladybugs hibernate when the weather gets cool. Count the dots on each ladybug wing. Then write an equation to show the total number of dots each ladybug has. The first one has been done for you.

    __3__ + __3__ = __6__

    _____ + _____ = _____

    _____ + _____ = _____

    _____ + _____ = _____

    _____ + _____ = _____

    _____ + _____ = _____

Write the sums in order, from lowest to highest.

_____ _____ _____ _____ _____

What pattern do you see?

_____

Not Far From Home

Start at ⌂ . Write the number of steps. Add.

steps to + steps home = _____ steps

steps to + steps home = _____ steps

_7_ + _7_ = _14_

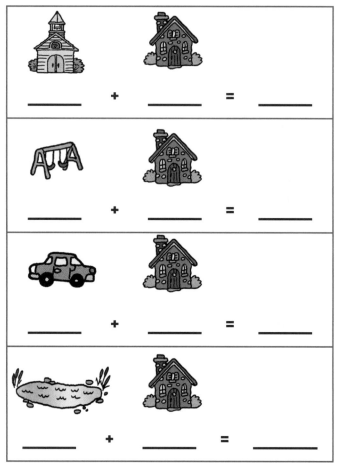

The Big Search

Subtract. Circle the difference.

11 – 7 = five three (four)	**14 – 9 =** nine one five
13 – 6 = six nine seven	**16 – 5 =** twelve thirteen eleven
18 – 9 = eleven ten nine	**17 – 11 =** seven six ten
15 – 5 = ten seven five	**12 – 9 =** three two four
12 – 4 = six eight nine	**11 – 9 =** three five two

Find each circled number in the word puzzle. Look → and ↓.

```
( f  o  u  r )  h    i    o    n    e    g    s    k    m
  i    f    o    n    t    g    y    f    a    f    u    e    z
  f    t    l    u    e    j    s    i    x    s    b    x    t
  t    t    w    e    l    v    e    v    k    s    t    l    h
  e    p    n    i    n    e    w    e    j    e    r    t    i
  e    d    n    g    q    i    h    r    y    v    a    q    r
  n    v    h    h    o    t    h    r    e    e    c    s    t
  d    m    k    t    c    w    b    t    e    n    t    r    e
  x    d    i    p    g    o    a    c    p    f    i    s    e
  c    e    l    e    v    e    n    a    b    z    o    v    n
  b    w    u    d    i    f    f    e    r    e    n    c    e
```

 See if you can find these number words: *twelve, fifteen, thirteen, subtraction, difference.*

Race Through the Facts

Add or subtract. The race car that ends with the highest number wins the race!

7 + 2 = ____   – 4 = ____   – 3 = ____   + 9 = ____   + 5 = ____

12 – 3 = ____   – 6 = ____   + 2 = ____   + 9 = ____   – 6 = ____   – 8 = ____

+ 4 = ____   + 7 = ____   – 6 = ____   + 3 = ____   – 2 = ____   + 7 = ____

+ 6 = ____   – 9 = ____   + 1 = ____   + 4 = ____   + 1 = ____

+ 1 = ____   – 8 = ____   + 2 = ____   + 3 = ____   – 3 = ____

– 11 = ____   – 5 = ____   + 13 = ____   – 7 = ____   + 3 = ____

Color the winning race car blue.

Little Snacks

Add or subtract. Then follow the maze through the even answers.

Start

$13 - 6 =$

$16 - 9 =$

$4 + 5 =$

$2 + 2 =$

$14 - 8 =$

$10 - 7 =$

$13 - 5 =$

$3 + 7 =$

$9 + 4 =$

$15 - 6 =$

$16 - 6 =$

$11 + 3 =$

$17 - 8 =$

$7 + 5 =$

$18 - 6 =$

$5 + 2 =$

$8 + 3 =$

$9 + 9 =$

The elephant found 9 peanuts. He ate 6 peanuts.

How many peanuts are left? _____

The Truth About the Tooth Fairy

Look at Ali Gator's teeth.

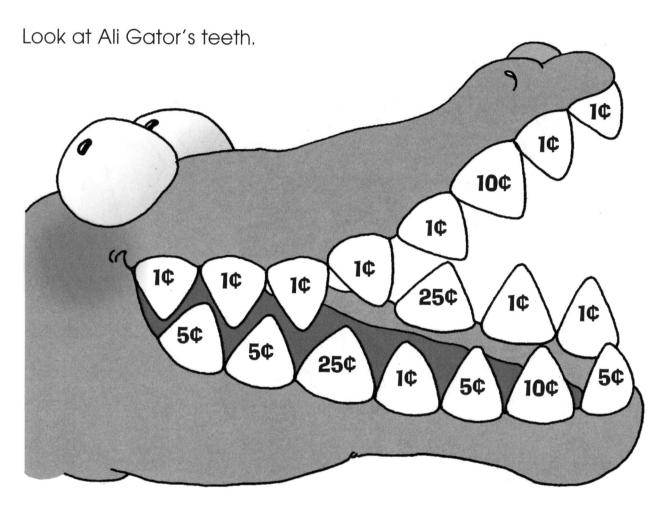

	How many teeth?	How much money in all?
1. How many 1¢?		cents
2. How many 5¢?		cents
3. How many 10¢?		cents
4. How many 25¢?		cents

Clock Work

Draw the hands on the clock so it shows 2:00.

Draw the hands on the clock so it shows 3:00.

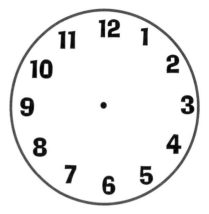

Draw the hands on the clock so it shows 4:00.

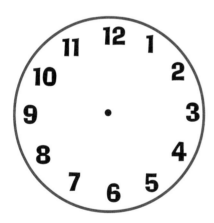

Draw the hands on the clock so it shows 5:00.

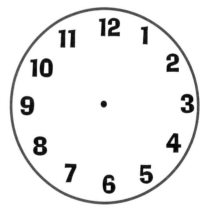

What do you do at 2:00 in the afternoon?

Write about it on the lines below.

_____

_____

More Clock Work

Draw the hands on the clock so it shows 3:30.

Draw the hands on the clock so it shows 7:30.

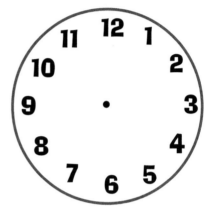

Draw the hands on the clock so it shows 9:30.

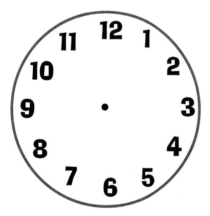

Draw the hands on the clock so it shows 1:30.

What do you do at 3:30 in the afternoon?

Write about it on the lines below.

_____

_____

About Time

Why do we need to know how to tell time? List your ideas below.

_____

_____

_____

How Long Is a Minute?

Think about how much you can do in one minute.
Write your estimates in the Prediction column. Then time yourself.
Write the actual number in the Result column.

Prediction: In One Minute I Can . . .	Result
Jump rope _____ times.	
Write the numbers 1 to _____ .	
Say the names of _____ animals.	

Answer Key

Page 5
Answers will vary, but check to make sure that child has supplied correct numbers for each category.

Page 6
Check child's picture to make sure that each shape has the correct color: one = green; two = yellow; three = red; four = purple; five = blue.

Page 7
Check child's picture to make sure each shape has the correct color: 6 = yellow; 7 = green; 8 = brown; 9 = red; 10 = orange.

Page 8
A gecko

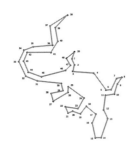

Page 9
No.

Check to make sure that child has drawn lines from five different frogs to the lily pads.

Extra: 2

Page 10
1. Answers will vary.

2. Numbers will be colored in using an AB pattern of red and blue.

Page 11
Yield sign: triangle, 3

Caution sign: diamond, 4

Speed-limit sign: rectangle, 4

Stop sign: octagon, 8

Page 12
Left birdhouse: cube, octagon, hexagon, rectangle, square, rectangle solid

Right birdhouse: cylinder, triangle, circle, rectangle

Page 13
Color the first butterfly, the second heart, the lightbulb, and the snowflake; drawings should show the other halves.

Page 14
5; child's patterns and equations will vary.

Page 15
$1 + 2 = 3$, $2 + 3 = 5$, $7 + 3 = 10$; $3 + 4 = 7$, $1 + 0 = 1$, $3 + 2 = 5$; $1 + 1 = 2$, $4 + 4 = 8$; $1 + 3 = 4$; The ladybug with 10 spots should be colored red. The ladybug with 1 spot should be colored blue.

Page 16

Check child's coloring.

Page 17
Check that the child has drawn the correct number of flowers. 7: needs 3; 10: needs 5; 4: needs 1; 6: needs 2, 9: needs 5; 5: needs 3; 8: needs 4; 3: needs 2; Color the bows with the numbers 4, 6, 8, and 10 yellow. Color the bows with 3, 5, 7, and 9 purple.

Page 18
A SAXOPHONE

$6 + 2 = 8$; $5 + 1 = 6$; $4 + 4 = 8$;

$3 + 6 = 9$; $3 + 0 = 3$; $3 + 4 = 7$;

$2 + 2 = 4$; $2 + 1 = 3$; $1 + 1 = 2$;

$0 + 1 = 1$

Page 19
$3 - 1 = 2$; $7 - 4 = 3$; $4 - 2 = 2$; $9 - 6 = 3$; $5 - 3 = 2$; $6 - 5 = 1$

Page 20
$5 - 3 = 2$; $7 - 4 = 3$; $10 - 5 = 5$; $9 - 2 = 7$; $8 - 7 = 1$; $9 - 6 = 3$; $6 - 1 = 5$; $10 - 2 = 8$; $7 - 5 = 2$; $5 - 1 = 4$; $8 - 2 = 6$; $8 - 0 = 8$; $9 - 7 = 2$; $8 - 5 = 3$; $10 - 4 = 6$; $10 - 3 = 7$; $9 - 4 = 5$; $8 - 1 = 7$; $6 - 4 = 2$; $6 - 3 = 3$; $7 - 2 = 5$; $9 - 0 = 9$; $10 - 1 = 9$

Page 21

Page 22

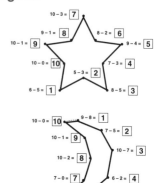

Page 23
Answers will vary.

Page 24
3 1/2 inches, 2 inches, 1 1/2 inches, 3 inches

Patty, Peter, Petunia, Paul

Page 25
pencil: 2
lunchbox: 1
crayon: 2
notebook: 1

Page 26
book height: 2 centimeters
book width: 3 centimeters
straw: 6 centimeters
marker: 4 centimeters
5 cubes: 4 centimeters
10 cubes: 8 centimeters
shoe: 5 centimeters
hand: 3 centimeters

Page 27
7 − 3 = 4; 9 − 6 = 3; 2 + 0 = 2;
5 + 5 = 10; 8 − 7 = 1; 4 + 3 = 7;
10 − 4 = 6; 6 + 2 = 8; 7 − 2 = 5;
The rabbit moved right to add. The
rabbit moved left to subtract.

Page 28

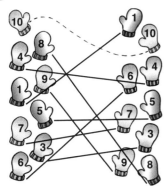

Page 29

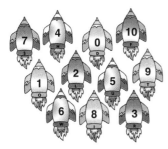

IT'S OUT OF THIS WORLD!

Page 30
A. 6 + 4 = 10; B. 10 − 5 = 5; C. 9 − 2
= 7; D. 4 + 6 = 10; E. 7 + 2 = 9; F. 2
+ 3 = 5; G. 5 + 3 = 8; H. 6 + 4 = 10;
I. 8 − 7 = 1; J. 10 − 3 = 7

Page 31
A. 7 + 3 = 10; B. 7 − 4 = 3; C. 10 − 6
= 4; D. 8 − 2 = 6; E. 5 + 4 = 9

Page 32

A. 6 + 2 = 8; B. 3 + 1 = 4;
C. 6 − 4 = 2

Page 33
Answers will vary. The following is a
likely answer. Check child's graph to
make sure that it corresponds to the
boxes checked.
chicken: see, hear, smell, touch
sun: see
lemonade: see, touch, taste
flowers: see, smell, touch
drums: see, hear, touch

Page 34
Answers will vary.

Page 35

7 leaps

Page 36
Beans talk.
4 + 2 = 6; 7 + 7 = 14; 9 + 5 = 14;
10 + 4 = 14; 4 + 8 = 12; 6 + 8 = 14;
11 + 3 = 14; 14 + 0 = 14; 7 + 2 = 9;
13 + 1 = 14; 5 + 8 = 13; 12 + 2 = 14;
7 + 4 = 11; 5 + 9 = 14

Page 37
4 + 4 = 8
5 + 5 = 10
6 + 6 = 12
7 + 7 = 14
8 + 8 = 16
Extra: 6, 8, 10, 12, 14, 16
Pattern: Count by 2s, even
numbers, doubling

Page 38
7 + 7 = 14; 6 + 6 = 12; 8 + 8 = 16;
9 + 9 = 18; 10 + 10 = 20; 4 + 4 = 8;
3 + 3 = 6; 5 + 5 = 10

Page 39
four, five; seven, eleven; nine, six;
ten, three; eight, two

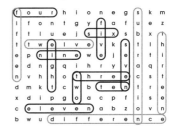

Page 40
7 + 2 = **9** − 4 = **5** − 3 = **2** + 9 = **11** +
5 = **16** − 8 = **8** + 4 = **12** + 6 = **18** − 9
= **9** + 1 = **10** + 4 = **14** − 8 = **6** + 2 =
8 + 3 = **11** − 3 = **8**; 12 − 3 = **9** − 6 =
3 + 2 = **5** + 9 = **14** − 6 = **8** + 7 = **15** −
6 = **9** + 3 = **12** − 2 = **10** + 7 = **17** + 1
= **18** − 11 = **7** − 5 = **2** + 13 = **15** − 7
= **8** + 3 = **11**; Color the bottom car
blue.

Page 41

3 peanuts

Page 42

1¢: 10 coins for 10¢

5¢: 4 coins for 20¢

10¢: 2 coins for 20¢

25¢: 2 coins for 50¢

Page 43

Page 44

Page 45

Answers will vary.